THEN AND NOW

FOREWORD

Every picture, so they say, is worth a thousand words and that is certainly true of this book, which takes the simple premise that the streets of Darlington have changed dramatically down the years and that the best way to portray those changes is through photography.

For this book, we have kindly been given permission to use photographs from the archives of The Northern Echo, which has been chronicling the life of the town for more than 100 years, in order to re-create scenes of yesteryear. The result is a stroll round the town which allows us to see how it has evolved.

The pictures were not selected to represent a particular era. Some date back to the 1870s, others are as recent as forty years ago, but they all have something in common: they take a moment in time and offer us the chance to see how streets have changed. In some cases, they show how streets have undergone remarkably little change despite the passage of time, in others the transformation is truly amazing.

I have made every effort to re-shoot the pictures from the places where the originals were taken. However, sometimes it was difficult to identify where the original photographer was standing, because original buildings have disappeared. The key to recreating the pictures was to identify surviving landmarks, for which houses, churches, shops, towers and even trees came in useful.

Whatever the challenges, Darlington Then and Now provides a snapshot of a town which is changing, sometimes for the better, sometimes, it could be argued, for the worst. The better is represented by some of the developments which have added to the town's character, the worst by those which have eradicated attractive buildings to make way for ugly creations.

The difference - and it is only a personal view - is that the better are those cases in which sensitivity and respect for the past has been shown in coming up with designs for the future. In some cases, streets have been greatly enhanced by the skill of modern architects and town planners: in others, their character has been eradicated by carbuncles - as Prince Charles might say - made of concrete, tarmac and lack of creativity.

The debate on which is which will continue for many years yet but the one thing which has not changed, and on which we can all agree, is the dramatic impact of the motor car. Once-quiet streets have been transformed into busy thoroughfares full of traffic fumes and rushing cars, buses and lorries. And even though the modern pictures were taken at the quietest time of the week, the presence of cars was nevertheless felt even on a Sunday, both in the dramatic increase in traffic and in the veritable forest of signs and bollards which it has spawned. They may be necessary but it is hard to escape the feeling that, in some instances, they have wrecked once-elegant street scenes.

Throughout the book, there are Darlington fact files. They do not necessarily relate to the street featured on the page but are there to provide snippets of interest about the town.

One final point: this book does not set out to be a comprehensive history of the town. I happily leave that function to others better qualified than myself to write such works. What it is meant to do, however, is, perhaps, make us pause a moment and think about the changes that are happening to our town - and take a greater, more proactive, interest in them when 'progress' threatens something special.

John Dean
September 2004

DARLINGTON THEN AND NOW

By John Dean

Copyright© John Dean 2004

The right of John Dean to be identified as the Author of this work has been asserted by him in accordance with the Copyright, Designs and Patents Act 1988.

All rights reserved.
This book is sold subject to the condition that it shall not, by way of trade or otherwise, be lent, resold, hired out or otherwise circulated without the publisher's prior consent in any form of binding or cover other than that in which it is published and without a similar condition including this condition being imposed on the subsequent purchaser.
First published in the United Kingdom, in 2004 by Inscribe Media Limited and Pro-Actif Communications, both of Darlington
For further information about the book contact John Dean at deangriss@btinternet.com

ISBN 0-9548343-0-5

Front page picture: Duplex Motor and Cycle Co in Grange Road

1962

We start our stroll round old Darlington on the northern fringes of the town, at **HARROWGATE HILL**. This is North Road, pictured in 1962 from its junction with Lowson Street. On the right of this picture is St Mark's church, which is still there today. At first glance, the picture seems to show an area which has not changed dramatically - until you think of what is happening just out of shot. The junction with Salters Lane North, for instance, has recently been redeveoped for housing and just round the corner, meadows have given way to the large Whinfield housing estate.

Fact File

In 1904, Darlington Corporation Light Railway opened and the first tramcars went to Harrowgate Hill. The system was closed down in 1926

1960

Walking further down **NORTH ROAD** we come across a scene which was familiar for many years and which has now, sadly, been lost for ever. Indeed, it could so easily symbolise the demise of traditional industries the region over. The picture, taken in 1960, shows workmen leaving North Road railway shops, one of the most important locomotive centres in Britain in its heyday. Within six years, however, the shops had closed and thousands of men had lost their jobs. Today, the only evidence the works were ever there is the old clock, mounted on the wall of the Morrisons superstore which stands on the site. St Paul's Church, which stood near the works and was built in 1872, was destroyed by fire in 1973 and demolished, stone by stone to avoid threatening nearby houses, a year later.

Fact File

North Road Engine Works opened in 1863, providing work for thousands, and closed a century later

1964

On the way into town we walk along **CORPORATION ROAD**, pictured here in 1964 from the hospital end. The Methodist Church dominated the street scene when this picture was taken but within five years it had been demolished. Today, the site is a housing development. For all that, although there have been changes, it is a street which can still be recognised today. The first building on the left, for example, is, then as now, the Old Vicarage, seen here largely obscured from view by the tree.

Fact File

Construction work on St Cuthbert's Church was started in about 1192. Building finally finished in the middle of the 13th century

1962

On our way into town from Corporation Road, we take a diversion along Gladstone Street and into **NORTH LODGE TERRACE**, pictured in 1962. Many people will remember the swimming baths, long since closed down and replaced by the pool in the Dolphin Centre. Gladstone Street can still be recognised today although the old Central School is now occupied by the community safety department rather than lively schoolchildren. Although the park and North Lodge Terrace are instantly recognisable the street seems somehow more cluttered these days.

Fact File

Darlington covered market was erected in 1863 with the cattle market opened in 1878

1897

Further back in time and we stroll along **NORTHGATE**, on the edge of the town centre, in 1897, the year the Technical College opened. The Bulmer stone (inset) can clearly be seen in the forefront of the picture. Carried down by a glacier, it remained in the same spot as the street developed around it. In 1923, having stood on the edge of the pavement it was placed behind railings because it was a hazard to traffic. The street has changed - for a start, there are a lot more vehicles and Northgate is packed with takeaways - but some constants remain. As ever, the stone is still there, behind its railings, and on the right side of the road are the Northgate United Reformed Church and the Salvation Army Citadel.

Fact File

Darlington Railway Centre and Museum, in North Road, dates back to 1842 when it was a station on the original route of the Stockton and Darlington railway, which became the world's first public steam railway in 1825

1950

It is the 1950s and we are in one of the streets which shows the most dramatic change. Half a century ago, **COMMERCIAL STREET** was a residential thriving street with lives enacted in its terraced homes but today it is part of the town centre, home to the huge monolithic building that is Regent House, and, nearby, The Lounge night-spot. However, there are further plans to demolish what is there now to make way for a new shopping centre. Yet another chapter in the life of Commercial Street.

Fact File

Firebrand Methodist preacher John Wesley first preached in Darlington in 1761 when worshippers met in a small house near the current site of the Cricketers hotel. When he came back in 1777, they had moved to a rented room opposite the Sun Inn in Northgate

1890

We head into **BONDGATE**, pausing to enjoy a scene from the 1890s. Once one of Darlington's most impressive streets, Bondgate was a wide cobbled thoroughfare with a certain elegance. Today, it seems narrower thanks to the street furniture and the pedestrian crossings and there is a large roundabout which is part of the inner ring road, necessary as part of modern traffic management but not exactly gladdening to the eye. Sadly, although the street retains some pleasant shopfronts, some have been replaced by more modern, garish ones. A glance at the rooftops shows how the street once was, leaving a sense of a spirit which has somehow been lost.

Fact File

The Nag's Head pub, in Tubwell Row, was the site of a vicarage in Tudor times. The pub was rebuilt in 1962/3 and is still there.

1900

HIGH ROW in the early 1900s, a fascinating picture which shows a bustling street with canopies, cobbles, atmospheric shopfronts and cows brought in for market. As the prime shopping street in the town, High Row has undergone plenty of change over the years. Most changes have been structural, the wide sloping street divided into two and forested with roads signs, barriers and bus stops ... and the cows tend not to venture along High Row any more! But for all that, the sense of history has been preserved and the street is instantly recognisable.

Fact File

Darlington existed at least as far back as Saxon times although evidence for Roman or prehistoric occupation remains far sketchier. There was, of course, a Roman fort at Piercebridge

1870

We pop down **TUBWELL ROW**, pictured in the 1870s and another street which is still recognisable despite the many changes it has undergone down the ages. It is almost as wide as ever and the market hall remains as do some of the buildings skirting the market place. However, there is one significant change because a number of buildings on the left hand side were demolished to make way for the Cornmill Centre, which opened in 1992.

Fact File

The Northern Echo, Darlington's morning paper, started life as the country's first half pence morning newspaper, opened by Hyslop Bell in 1870 and printed in Penny Yard, Priestgate

1964

Across into **PRIESTGATE**, home of The Northern Echo for more than a century. This picture was taken in 1964 and although much of the street can still be recognised, there have been huge changes. The Co-Operative store has gone and in its place is one of the entrances to the Cornmill Centre with its bridge across the road, creating the impression of a street viewed through a tunnel. Right at the top of Priestgate, the Red Lion continues to serve pints to its regulars although these days Skinnergate is the main focus of weekend nightlife.

Fact File

Famous editors of The Northern Echo down the ages have included pioneering journalist W T Stead, its second editor in 1871, and Harold Evans, who went on to edit The Sunday Times and is now working and living in the US

1920

Turning the clock back more than 80 years, we are in **BLACKWELLGATE** in the 1920s. The picture, complete with old cars and bicycles, shows a wide atmospheric street packed with character. Today, much of its character has been retained and many of the buildings remain the same even if the owners have changed, places like the much-loved Green Tree cafe having closed.

Fact File

Darlington Football Club was founded in 1883 and, until its recent move to a new stadium on Neasham Road, had spent its entire history at Feethams

1963

Fast forward to **SKINNERGATE** in 1963, easily recognisable but with plenty of changes if you look closely. Halfords, on the left, went recently, Uptons is long gone and the street is now pedestrianised for much of the day. But the main change has been the life of the street at night: the traditional pubs like The Bowes, the old heavy rockers' haunt, have changed their names and character several times and new hostelries have opened, and re-opened, at a bewildering rate, making Skinnergate the hub of Darlington at night, particularly on a weekend.

Fact File

Pease's Mill was a major landmark in the town centre. It closed in 1972, was demolished in 1984 and is now the site of a car park

1920

We are in **GRANGE ROAD**, in the town centre, in the 1920s and a fascinating picture showing the Duplex Motor and Cycle Company. Duplex was a hugely important name in the town, selling bicycles as far back as the 1800s. The Duplex Motor and Cycle Co. occupied nearly all of the west side of Grange Road in the town centre, having been founded by Tommy Alston, who died in 1956. By the time of his death he had seen it expand onto the other side of the road as well. Having come to the town at the age of 14 and become apprenticed to his uncle, a draper, he pawned his overcoat in 1903 to buy a bike for 15s, later moving into motorbikes. Duplex lasted until the late-Sixties. Today, this part of Grange Road is home to specialist stores which give the town centre an added attraction.

Fact File

In 1841 the Great North of England Railway opened, linking York with Darlington's Bank Top station

1951

DUKE STREET in 1951. Like many streets in the town, it can be easily recognised. One of the big changes was the construction of a traffic roundabout where Duke Street meets Abbey Road and Stanhope Road - necessary to accommodate increased traffic but one can't help feel it detracted from the elegant sweep of the street up towards what is now the sixth form college.

Fact File

Darlington Library, then the Edward Pease Public Library, was opened in 1885 after Edward Pease left £10,000 for the work. It was extended in 1933

1963

We head from Duke Street into **LARCHFIELD STREET**, towards its junction with Coniscliffe Road, recognisable in 1963 but having undergone change over the last 40 years. The main changes were brought about by the inner ring road, which opened in the mid-seventies and turned this corner into a busy junction because it is just yards from the large Grange Road roundabout.

Fact File

St Augustine's Church, which is hidden away behind Coniscliffe Road, was opened in 1827

Post-War

Walking further along **CONISCLIFFE ROAD**, only a short distance, we come to a picture of unknown date but probably in the post-war years. In those days, as Britain returned to normal, there were still few cars around and this junction with Cleveland Terrace was considerably quieter in those days. Contrast that with the busy scene today.

Fact File

Darlington bus station was opened in 1961. The nearby town hall was opened in 1969

1900s

A fascinating photograph of **LINDEN AVENUE**, date unknown but some time in the 20th century. It shows the dramatic change in a street which lies at the heart of the West End. A couple of centuries ago, Carmel Road was the town's unofficial frontier, separating the meadows on the road to Barnard Castle from the beginnings of the built-up area and the large homes of industrialists, which were being constructed as the 19th century approached its end. This picture was taken from the Coniscliffe Road end of the avenue and on the left in the forefront can be seen the wall to The Knoll, one of the most imposing houses in the area. It was built by the Church Commissioners in 1860 and is still there today.

Fact File

Central Hall in the Market Place was opened in 1847 and included a hall, library and committee rooms. After a history including time as a concert hall, theatre and cinema, it closed in 1946 but is now part of the Dolphin Centre

1900s

COCKERTON GREEN, taken from the end nearest the shops, back in the days when the National School was still operating. Built in 1825 and extended at least four times, the school catered for infants, junior and senior scholars but by 1925 only the latter remained because the others had gone to St Mary's School, now Carmel school. The seniors stayed at the National School until 1949 and the building itself was demolished in 1960. Today the village centre is extremely busy with a shopping area and library.

Fact File

Hopetown railway works, close to North Road Railway Centre and Museum, dates back to 1853 and is used for the construction, by a trust, of the Tornado, a LNER Peppercorn Class A1 Pacific, the first mainline steam engine to be built in this country for four decades

1800s

We continue our stroll and head back into town along **WOODLAND ROAD**, which 150 years ago was still just a country lane with a stream running down the middle of it but was, even then, developing fast. Holy Trinity Church, with its tower was built in 1836. Nearby was a mansion called Woodlands, built about 1829.

Fact File

Carmel Convent, in Nunnery Lane, dates back to 1830, the church being consecrated in 1859

1950

MILBANK ROAD in the 1950s. The road owes its existence to the decision by Lord Barnard around the turn of the 19th century to sell off some of his vast tracts of land. In the road's early days it was called Thornton's Lonin (Lane) but Milbank may have been chosen in tribute to former landowners, the Milbankes, who bought a lot of land in Darlington in 1700. Or it could be in appreciation of Mark Milbanke of Bedale who married Lord Barnard's third daughter, Augusta-Henrietta, in 1817.

Fact File

The first Darlington school to provide proper education for the poor was St Cuthbert's School, established in 1812, closed, after moving to the Leadyard, in 1931

1930

Heading back across town, down **VICTORIA ROAD** in the 1930s, when the whole area was still a warren of side streets. The 1970s brought great change as a large house clearance programme allowed the inner ring road to cut through Victoria Road. Although necessary to cope with the growing amount of traffic, there are nevertheless those who feel that the loss of all those streets robbed the area of much of its character. Today, where people once lived their lives, are offices, shops, a supermarket and a filling station.

Fact File

Bank Top station, the town's main railway station, was opened in 1887 and was designed by architect W. Bell

1971

No prizes for guessing the big change in this picture of **EAST MOUNT ROAD**, off Haughton Road. In 1971, when this picture was taken, Darlington Power Station was still operating and its chimneys and cooling towers dominated the skyline. That was soon to change: opened in 1900 and modernised in 1939, the power station closed in 1976, having employed 123 people. The towers and chimneys were subsequently demolished and the skyline was never the same.

Fact File

Feethams, until latterly home to Darlington Football Club and still used for cricket, was once a field. Nearby was Bishop's Mill, which was demolished in 1966

1971

HAUGHTON ROAD in 1971 and a sad reminder of a lost friend. It was in 1998 that the Havelock Arms, on the edge of Albert Hill, closed having occupied the Barton Street corner site for at least 120 years. The site had history because one of three tunnels leading from the Havelock's cellars led to an old brewery, where the petrol station stands. The South Durham Brewery Company began during the 1880s and was renamed the Haughton Road Brewery in 1894 when purchased by Thomas Clayhills. The Havelock dated from the 1860s, possibly earlier, and was probably rebuilt by Clayhills in 1894. The Haughton Road Brewery was demolished just before the Second World War and following its closure in 1998, the Havelock went the same way.

Fact File

The Havelock pub, in Haughtion Road, was demolished following its closure in 1998, which made the derelict building a victim of vandals and arsonists

1971

NEASHAM ROAD in 1971 and a man cleans up after a spillage of some sort. The street has undergone some dramatic changes. Until 1980 it was the home for businesses established by entrepreneur William Richardson in 1874, who constructed glasshouses and opened the North of England Horticultural Works off Neasham Road. After changing hands, the works had to be rebuilt in 1960 after a large fire. Production finished there in 1980, the site was cleared in 1987 and today it is home to a Matalan superstore and another new retail development. St John's Church, at the junction with Parkgate/Yarm Road is still standing, of course.

Fact File

Diesel vehicles replaced trolley buses in Darlington in 1951 although the last trolley bus trundled on until 1957

1962

EASTBOURNE ROAD and a street which has changed little. These pictures are taken looking down towards Neasham Road, with the railway station in the background. Take a few steps forward along Eastbourne Road and the clock tower comes into view.

Fact File

The Stockton & Darlington Railway, formed in 1825, remained independent until in 1863 when it was swallowed up by North Eastern Railway (NER)

1920

We make the short journey to **YARM ROAD**, and its junction with Hundens Lane, and a picture taken in 1920. Interestingly, the name Thomas Clayhills, he of Haughton Brewery and Havelock fame, pops up here as well because at one time the Clayhills empire owned the Hope, one of 41 pubs and 11 off-licences which they owned. Next to the pub, to the left as we look, was one of the grimmest buildings in Darlington, the old workhouse, built in 1869. When it opened on June 1, 1870, 117 paupers were moved there from the derelict workhouse in Leadyard. Over the years, it had various names: Darlington Union Workhouse, the New Feetham Institute, Eastbourne Hospital and East Haven. In 1974, when the building closed, it was providing shelter for the homeless and nursing for geriatric patients. After its demolition it became open space, popular with dog walkers, but today it has been redeveloped for residential purposes. The Hope springs eternal, of course.

Fact File

The name Darlington, which means tun, for village or homestead, of Deornod's people, has been spelled Dearthington, Dearnington, Dearington, Dernington, Darington, Darnton and Derlington at various times in its history

1896

Time for a stroll in the park. Darlington Borough Council has spent nearly £4m of National Lottery money to restore **SOUTH PARK**, which has an important place in history. Created on a site known as the Poor Howdens, it was a response to the disease-ridden sanitary conditions in Darlington's terraced streets as the town developed as an industrial centre. The first such municipal parks in the north were in Sheffield (1841) and Liverpool (1842) but Darlington was the first in the North-East. Planning began in 1851 and the result was a park of true Victorian splendour with trees and promenades. The recent investment has started the process of regaining the park's lost glories, much tarnished by years of neglect and attacks by vandals. This picture shows the park in its heyday with the bandstand, pictured in 1896. Today, much of it is recognisable although the bandstand is more enclosed by steps and trees than in this picture.

Fact File

The teahouse in South Park was officially opened in 1908 at a ceremony attended by the mayor and mayoress.

1987

SNIPE LANE in 1987: by far the most recent 'old picture' in this book but included because the road had undergone more change than most. Until the 1980s, it was a quiet backwater nestling in farmland on the southern fringe of the town. Then in the mid-eighties, the five-mile long £5.6m Darlington bypass opened, running from Blands Corner to Great Burdon and designed to give Teesside commercial traffic an easy route to the A1 without clogging up areas like Haughton village in Darlington. Snipe Lane remains secluded behind tall hedges and trees but just metres away, vehicles thunder past at 70mph.

Fact File

The Darlington A66 bypass road was opened in 1985, designed to take Teesside traffic direct to the A1

Bibliography

- Echo Memories, the long-running series of local history articles printed in The Northern Echo, as well as several books, written by Chris Lloyd

- Historic Darlington, by Edward Wooler and Alfred Caine Boyde, published by Sir Isaac Pitman and Sons Ltd, London, in 1913

- The Book of Darlington, written by George Flynn, published by Barracuda Books Limited, in 1987

- Darlington As It Was, written by S C Dean and U M Clough, published by Hendon Publishing Co Ltd, in 1974

- Darlington in the 1930s and '40s, written by Doreen and Stan Dean, published by Hendon Publishing, in 1984